Homophone

Words That Sound Alike

Confusing Words to Search and Find Easily

by

Intellectually Competitive Edge, Inc.

ISBN: 978-1-931450-06-5

Acknowledgement

Thank you to all past, current, and future teachers of language, spelling, and grammar for realizing that communication is the essence of human relations.

Who Could Use This Book

This reference book is especially for any and every person who wants to improve their (or someone else's) understanding of the American English language.

This reference book is also for people who communicate through writing and who do not want the recipient be distracted by typos.

This is the perfect gift for:

- Parents to help their children.
- Teachers to pass on to their students.
- ESL students to help themselves.
- Employers who want their employees to succeed.
- Guidance counselors who want their students to succeed.
- Anyone writing essays to accompany entrance applications.
- Employees who want their written communications to be taken seriously.

How to Use This Book

The best way to use this book is to:

Write your email, letter, essay, book report, thesis, novel, or any other correspondence without worrying about the words that confuse you. Simply remain focused on your larger task – whatever it is you are writing.

Find the word that confuses you after you have finished writing. Use any of the following methods:

- the Table of Pronunciations, sounding out the word you are thinking of;
- the Index of Word Groups, locating the word you know how to spell; or
- dictionary style, looking at the top of the pages while flipping through the sets of words, which are alphabetized within each group, which is then alphabetized accordingly among the other groups.

Understand which of the words within the group is the correct one, and edit your writing accordingly.

How to Use the Table of Pronunciations

This book is designed to be easy to use, including finding the words that confuse you. Common words are listed below followed by the easiest phonetic representation possible of the bolded letter. All CAPS is where the word is typically emphasized.

As in...	Pronounced
ale	ay
all	ah
ask	ehah
assemble	eh
eel	ee
eliminate	eh
I	i
ignore	ih
irk	uh
oak	oh
olive	ah
order	oo
ounce	ow
unique	yuw
under	uh
uber	uw
shin	sh (as usual)
thin	th (as usual)
w**oo**d	wuhd

Table of Pronunciations

acts • axe

Max uses a plastic ***axe*** on stage when he ***acts*** as a young George Washington chopping down a cherry tree.

acts	to presently perform.
axe	a tool fitted with a steel cutting head.

ad • add

Brad places an ***ad*** in the local newspaper to ***add*** to his list of business clients.

ad	an advertisement.
add	to join, unit, or combine.

ail • ale

Gail drinks the dark ***ale*** and begins to ***ail*** shortly after.

ail	to be slightly ill.
ale	an alcoholic beverage.

air • heir

Mary's father was an ***heir*** to untold fortunes her father acquired as a dare devil, whose claim to fame was working 500 feet in the ***air*** as a tightrope walker.

air	the atmosphere; the space above us.
heir	a person who is or will become the owner of another's property upon that other's death.

aisle • isle

Kyle visits the ***isle*** and sees the flowers that remind him of the ones adorning the church ***aisle*** at his sister's wedding last year.

aisle	a side division (of a church).
isle	a small island.

all • awl

Paul used an ***awl*** to puncture ***all*** along one edge of a leather strap.

all	the whole quantity of something.
awl	a short pointed tool used for making holes.

allowed • aloud

Howie's girlfriend ***allowed*** him to proclaim his love for her ***aloud*** at the baseball game, where he asked her to marry him.

allowed	to be or to have permitted to do.
aloud	speaking in a normal voice so as to be heard.

altar • alter

Walter kneeled before the ***altar*** at his church and vowed to ***alter*** his life for the better.

altar	a raised structure for offering sacrifices to a deity.
alter	to make different; to change.

ascent • assent

Madison made ***ascent*** to the platform where the dean stood, and her handshake was her ***assent*** for the dean to give her a well-deserved diploma.

ascent	the act of ascending; a climbing.
assent	an acceptance of a doctrine.

assistance • assistants

Misty gave her ***assistants*** flowers for all of the ***assistance*** they have given to her during the last two months.

assistance	a usefulness.
assistants	more than one helper.

ate • eight

Kate ***ate*** breakfast promptly at ***eight*** o'clock this morning.

ate	to have eaten.
eight	being one more than seven.

bail • bale

Gail paid her brother's ***bail*** when he was caught taking a ***bale*** of hay from the neighbor's farm.

bail	a money or property security deposit to obtain a prisoner's freedom.
bale	a tightly bound quantity of wheat, straw, cotton, etc.

ball • bawl

Paul began to ***bawl*** when he realized he tossed his ***ball*** over a high fence and into the neighbor's yard where he could not get it.

ball	a spherical object which is hit, kicked, thrown, etc.
bawl	to cry loudly and without restraint.

band • banned

Sandy's ***band*** was ***banned*** from performing at the festival because of the naughty lyrics in the songs the band performs.

band	a group of musicians playing together.
banned	to be or to have prohibited from a place or activity.

bare • bear

Claire walked through the woods in her ***bare*** feet and happened upon a ***bear***.

bare	uncovered; naked.
bear	a thick-furred, carnivorous mammal; to support.

baron • barren

Sharon's farmland is ***barren***, but she gladly inherited the land from her father, a ***baron***.

baron	a member of the lowest order of nobility.
barren	incapable of bearing (children, fruit, etc.).

base • bass

Jason likes his music with less treble and more ***bass***; to play the ***bass*** in music class; and to listen to his boom box at the ***base*** of the steps leading into his apartment building.

base	the bottom or lowest part of something.
bass	deep in tone or pitch; a musical instrument.

be • bee

Bea will ***be*** at a ***bee*** keeper's convention this week learning how to harvest these wonders of nature.

be	the state of being.
bee	a four-winged insect that produces was and honey.

beach • beech

Reese noticed the road leading to the ***beach*** had palm trees, not like the ***beech*** trees near her home.

beach	the shore of a sea or a lake.
beech	a genus of smooth gray-barked trees.

beat • beet

Pete grated a ***beet*** for his omelet recipe, into which he would ***beat*** an egg and other special ingredients.

beat	to strike deliberately and often; to strike repeatedly as to whip.
beet	a genus of fleshy root vegetables.

beau • bow

Flo's ***beau*** gave her a silk ***bow*** for her hair, and it matched the dress she wore for their lunch date.

beau	a man who is courting.
bow	a slipknot formed by doubling (a shoelace, a ribbon, etc.); a weapon.

berth • birth

Bertha's ***birth*** occurred on the train's ***berth*** while Bertha's mother was on her way to visit family for the holiday.

berth	a bunk in a ship or train.
birth	the event of being born.

billed • build

Jill wanted to ***build*** a house, so she asked her carpenter brother, who promptly ***billed*** her for his services afterwards.

billed	to be or to have charged for goods or services.
build	a shape of a body; to construct.

blew • blue

Lou watched as the ***blue*** sky disappeared beneath the clouds when the wind ***blew*** ever stronger.

blew	to have blown.
blue	a color between green and violet.

boar • bore

Lori thought her cousin was a ***bore*** until he told her he had wrestled a wild ***boar*** in Hawaii.

boar	a wild hog.
bore	an uninteresting person.

board • bored

Morton was ***bored*** and decided to ***board*** a train to the lumber store to buy a ***board*** to repair his window frame.

board	a piece of sawed lumber longer than it is wide; to make one's way onto (a ship, train, etc.).
bored	to suffer or having suffered boredom.

boarder • border

Jordan was a frequent train ***boarder*** who liked to cross the ***border*** from Delaware to Pennsylvania and back as he travelled to and from work.

boarder	one who boards.
border	an edge; an outer side.

bolder • boulder

Holder grew ever ***bolder*** as he grew older and was able to single-handedly move a ***boulder*** about his front lawn.

bolder	even more confident.
boulder	a large stone or mass of rock.

born • borne

Warren was ***born*** to a mother who'd ***borne*** more than her fair share of trials in life.

born	having come to life by birth.
borne	after bearing (supporting or gone through) something.

brake • break

Jake took a ***break*** from repairing the front ***brake*** on his bicycle.

brake	a device for diminishing or preventing motion.
break	an interruption.

breach • breech

Peaches wanted to ***breach*** her purchase of the ***breech***, which she mistakenly thought was used in a local war more than a century ago.

breach	the breaking of or to break a legal obligation.
breech	a part of a cannon.

bread • bred

Ted broke little pieces of ***bread*** to feed the new kittens that his cat ***bred*** last month.

bread	food made from flour.
bred	the past of breeding.

borough • burro • burrow

Pearl rode a ***burro*** through her ***borough*** right up to her neighbor's front yard, where she saw a gopher ***burrow*** from one side of the yard to the other.

borough	a municipal corporation resembling an incorporated town.
burro	a small donkey used as a pack animal.
burrow	to dig a hole underground.

but • butt

Dutton fell on his ***butt*** several times when he first was learning to ice skate, ***but*** he kept trying until he could stay upright.

but	only; merely.
butt	the object of; to strike with head or horns; an animal's backside.

buy • by • bye

Ty swung ***by*** his sister's room to say ***"Bye"*** and that he was on his way to ***buy*** their mom some flowers.

buy	to purchase.
by	near; close to.
bye	goodbye.

cache • cash

Nash knows where his computer's ***cache*** is, but doesn't know where he put the ***cash*** his mother gave to him last night.

cache	a place to hide treasures.
cash	money in the form of coins or paper.

canvas • canvass

Candace went to ***canvass*** her neighborhood to determine how many artists wanted to participate in painting the largest oil painting on ***canvas*** her state has ever seen.

canvas	a strong, coarse cloth.
canvass	to seek votes.

capital • capitol

Apple went to the state ***capitol*** to view the constitution, a document that is spelled with a ***capital*** letter c.

capital	very great; having to do with wealth; in its relatively large form.
capitol	the building in which the state legislature meets.

carat • carrot

Carrie ate the ***carrot*** that she held with her left hand, where her ring finger held a quarter-***carat*** emerald ring.

carat	a measure of weight for gems.
carrot	a biennial plant whose root is used as a vegetable.

ceiling • sealing

Celia looked up at her living room ***ceiling*** fan and noticed the ***sealing*** around the base was coming off.

ceiling	the upper inner surface of a room.
sealing	having attached or marked with a seal.

cell • sell

Stella will ***sell*** her breakthrough skin ***cell*** formula at the beauty show this weekend.

cell	a small enclosed space; the smallest unit of living tissue that can function as an independent entity.
sell	to dispose of ownership of goods.

cellar • seller

Stella was a ***seller*** at the beauty show, and she took to the show some products she made in her ***cellar*** at home.

cellar	a room usually under a building used as a cool storage place.
seller	a person who sells.

cents • sense • scents

Millicent loved the ***scents*** of nature so she made candles with those same smells and sold them for two dollars and fifty ***cents*** each in order that people could ***sense*** the candles from their own homes.

cents	multiple hundredths of one U.S. dollar.
sense	hearing, sight, sound, smell, or touch; to perceive.
scents	smells.

cereal • serial

Celia was a ***serial*** eater of oat ***cereal***.

cereal	any of several plants whose seed is used for human food and for feeding livestock.
serial	forming or being arranged as a series.

chord • cord

Corey, before he struck his first ***chord*** on the piano, pulled the ***cord*** on the blinds so that the sun streamed in the room.

chord	a simultaneous combination of musical notes.
cord	a rope of small diameter.

cite • sight • site

Dwight enjoyed the ***sight*** of fellow students studying when he went to the library, a ***site*** that held books authored by his favorite scholars that he could ***cite*** for his upcoming book report.

cite	to quote an authority.
sight	the power of seeing.
site	the geographical location of.

coarse • course

Mrs. Morse used thick chalk on the ***coarse*** chalk board that occupied the room where she taught a ***course*** in marketing.

coarse	large-grained; not fine.
course	the direction of travel or path taken.

complacent • complaisant

Jason was ***complaisant*** with his father's choice of college, even though his father made the choice because he thought Jason was being ***complacent.***

complacent	self-satisfied.
complaisant	accepting of what others do without complaining.

complement • compliment

Dom's art work was a ***complement*** to the work of more established artists, and his first sale was a ***compliment*** to his talent.

complement	to complete.
compliment	a courteous praise.

council • counsel

Hansel provided ***counsel*** to the townspeople while he served on the town ***council***.

council	a consultative or advisory assembly.
counsel	the result of or to be given professional consultation.

cue • queue

Hugh used the ***cue*** to strike the next ball in ***queue*** and, when it did not go into the pocket, his friend took his ***cue*** that it was finally his turn to play.

cue	an agreed signal; a long leather-tipped rod for striking the ball in billiards.
queue	a line (of people) waiting their turn.

currant • current

Murray likes to eat one ***currant*** at a time on the dock with a mild ***current*** of water surrounding his feet, but at the ***current*** time it is raining outside.

currant	a genus of cold-climate fruits with berries.
current	of the present time; a mass of air, water or other fluid moving in a certain direction.

cymbal • symbol

Simpson learned that the ***cymbal*** was merely one ***symbol*** of big band music.

cymbal	one of a pair of sallow brass plates.
symbol	a sign or object representing a thing.

dear • deer

Vera was a ***dear*** who loved to feed ***deer*** in her yard.

dear	a loved or lovable person.
deer	a hoofed mammal.

dew • due • do

Lou liked to ***do*** what any boy does and wipe the ***dew*** from the flowers onto his chin, but he was ***due*** inside for breakfast.

dew	small drops of moisture.
due	expected to arrive.
do	to perform an action.

die • dye

Ty caused the flower to ***die*** when he chose to ***dye*** it orange, to match his favorite game ***die***.

die	to cease to live; a small cube marked on its face with 1 – 6 spots.
dye	to give color to; a substance capable of coloring materials.

discreet • discrete

Pete kept the potential buyers ***discrete***, and he promised them both that he'd be ***discreet*** about each respective transaction.

discreet	able to keep quiet about matters; not showy.
discrete	separate; distinct.

doe • dough

Joe was making ***dough*** when he noticed a ***doe*** just beyond his back deck.

doe	a female deer.
dough	a mass of slightly moistened flour.

dual • duel

Jewel had to ***duel*** her way through the ***dual***-headed monster in the video game.

dual	double.
duel	a fight.

eave • eve

Steve noticed the ***eave*** coming loose on the ***eve*** of his brother's wedding.

eave	a singular version of the part of a roof which projects over the top of a wall.
eve	the day before some named day.

ewe • you

Eunice has a ***ewe*** that she said ***you*** simply must see because it's so cute.

ewe	a female sheep.
you	the second person singular pronoun.

facts • fax

Max sent the ***fax*** earlier this morning with all the ***facts*** his sister needed about the case.

facts	things known to be true.
fax	as in facsimile.

fair • fare

Blair paid her ***fare*** to get to the August ***fair*** by the water.

Blair knew she would ***fare*** well at the games because she played ***fair***.

fair	according to the rules; a traveling collection of sideshows and amusements.
fare	the cost of a journey; to manage or get along.

faun • fawn

Dawn saw the ***fawn*** in her front lawn, and she recalled the story of the ***faun*** from her literature course.

faun	men with the horns, legs and tail of a goat and sharply pointed ears personifying fertility in nature in Roman mythology.
fawn	a young deer.

feat • feet

Pete accomplished quite a ***feat*** when he completed his gymnastics high bar routine by landing on both ***feet***.

feat	a deed.
feet	plural of a human body part; a unit of measure.

flair • flare

Claire had a ***flair*** for using the ***flare*** from the grill to make the best hamburgers.

flair	a natural ability; aptitude.
flare	a sudden emission of a bright flame.

flew • flue

Lou installed the chimney ***flue*** the day before he boarded an airplane and ***flew*** out of town.

flew	past tense of to fly.
flue	a pipe or vent for carrying smoke from inside to outside.

for • fore

Flora heard the player yell "**Fore!**" just after got to her spot ***for*** the golf match.

for	as a representative of; in support of.
fore	a warning to people in the line of flight of a golf ball.

foreword • forward

Lorna was standing in the bookstore line, but as she moved ***forward*** she read the ***foreword*** and was reduced to tears, so much so that she could not move ***forward*** with her afternoon without bawling.

foreword	a preface (of a book).
forward	toward the front; to advance or promote; in the direction that one is facing.

forth • fourth

George put ***forth*** his best effort, but he didn't put the golf ball in the hole until his ***fourth*** stroke.

forth	out from concealment.
fourth	being number four in a series.

gait • gate

Nate's horse attempted unsuccessfully to jump the ***gate***, and now the horse's ***gait*** has changed a bit.

gait	a manner of walking or running.
gate	a barrier on hinges capable of being opened and shut.

grate • great

Kate thought it would be ***great*** to be able to ***grate*** Parmesan cheese with her new kitchen tool.

grate	to reduce to small pieces by rubbing against a sharp surface.
great	large in size; big.

groan • grown

Grover emitted a ***groan*** when his blister had ***grown***, but he knew better than to pop it.

groan	to make a deep moaning sound through pain.
grown	having reached full size; to past of grow.

hair • hare

Claire had a ***hare*** that one day tried to eat the ***hair*** on her head as she picked it up to show her friends.

hair	threadlike tubal structure that is rooted in and grows from the skin.
hare	a rabbit.

heal • heel

Neal hurt his ***heel*** dancing, but now it is starting to ***heal***.

heal	to make or become well or whole again.
heel	the round part of a human foot.

hear • here

Vera came ***here*** today to ***hear*** what her professor had to say.

hear	to experience sound.
here	in this place.

hew • hue

Hugh preferred to ***hew*** at the crack of dawn, when the ***hue*** of the sky was not as brilliant.

hew	to cut by blows with an axe or other sharp-edged instrument.
hue	a quality of a color.

hoard • horde

Lourde owned an antique store, but she felt the need to ***hoard*** her favorite items from the ***horde*** that came through each day looking for her unique items.

hoard	to collect, keep, and store away.
horde	a vast number of people.

hole • whole

Joel wanted the ***hole*** he was digging for the post to be a ***whole*** lot bigger.

hole	a small space or cavity surrounding by matter.
whole	not lacking any part.

hour • our

Bower had one ***hour*** to get to the pizza shop to pickup ***our*** dinner before the shop closed.

hour	part of a solar day, subdivided into 60 minutes.
our	pertaining to or belonging to us.

intense • intents

Vincenta had all ***intents*** on remaining ***intense*** and not blinking an eye before her opponent did.

intense	very great; extreme.
intents	plural of one's concentrated attention.

knead • need

Dee said you ***need*** a firm hand to ***knead*** the dough evenly in order to make the best base for your pizza.

knead	to work dough or clay into a mass with the hands; to massage as if working dough.
need	to be in want.

knew • new

Lou ***knew*** that his shoes would not look ***new*** for long if he kept wearing them out in the rain.

knew	the result of knowing.
new	made, discovered, known, heard or seen for the first time.

knight • night

Dwight was the ***knight*** who rode all the way to the next town at ***night*** when he heard that his family was in trouble.

knight	a man given the rank of knighthood by the British monarch.
night	the time of the day which the sun is below the horizon.

knot • not

Scott did ***not*** want a ***knot*** in his shoe laces, so he asked his big sister to tie his shoes for him.

knot	a tangle of threads or strings.
not	used to express a negative.

know • no

Flo prefers to say "***No***," as you ***know***.

know	to apprehend with the conscious mind.
no	used to express lack, denial, or refusal; not any.

knows • nose

Joe's ***nose*** is so sensitive to smell that, even with his eyes closed, he ***knows*** the difference between the smell of dark chocolate and milk chocolate.

knows	as in he or she apprehending with the conscious mind.
nose	the facial feature above the mouth containing nostrils.

lead • led

Ned ***led*** his abatement team to where he found the ***lead*** paint so that they could remove it.

lead	a metallic element.
led	the result of showing the way, or leading.

lessen • lesson

Jessie took a ***lesson*** in cooking to ***lessen*** the burden on her mom.

lessen	to cause to become less.
lesson	something to be learned.

made • maid

Jade had a ***maid*** that always ***made*** the bed with the corners tucked in at the bottom.

made	result of making.
maid	a female domestic servant.

main • mane

Jane claimed her horse's ***mane*** was the ***main*** reason it attracted so much attention at shows.

main	the most important.
mane	the long hair growing on the top or sides of the neck of some animals.

marry • merry

Mary was very ***merry*** when her boyfriend asked her to ***marry*** him.

marry	to take in marriage.
merry	cheerful and happy.

meat • meet

Pete went to the ***meet*** and greet event, and he ate plenty of ***meat*** and potato salad.

meat	the flesh of animals.
meet	to come face-to-face with.

metal • mettle

Gretel earned a badge made of ***metal*** to symbolize her ***mettle*** during the most trying of times.

metal	an element, usually having luster, that are good conductors of heat and electricity.
mettle	spirit, courage, or fortitude.

might • mite

Dwight thinks he ***might*** have been bitten by more than one ***mite*** by the looks of the rash on his leg, and it took all of his ***might*** not to scratch the itch.

might	strength or power; an expression of a degree of possibility.
mite	tiny arachnids resembling ticks, only much smaller than ticks.

miner • minor

Mr. Kline was a ***miner*** but his role was not ***minor*** to his boss's.

miner	one who works in a mine.
minor	less in importance or size.

moat • mote

Cody saw many a ***mote*** by the light streaming into the room as he looked through the window and onto the ***moat*** around his lofty estate.

moat	a deep wide trench built around a fortification, castle, etc.
mote	a small particle (of dust floating in the air).

mold • mould

Joel was casting a ***mould*** out of clay when he noticed the ***mold*** in the mixture.

mold	a wooly or fluffy growth produced by various fungi.
mould	to make or form into a certain shape

moor • more

Lori was supposed to ***moor*** the boat to the dock before any ***more*** bad weather approached.

moor	to secure to the land or buoys by means of ropes.
more	greater in quantity, amount, or degree.

morning • mourning

Lorn was ***mourning*** the loss of her cat, so she took the ***morning*** off from her chores.

morning	the early part of the day between midnight or dawn and noon.
mourning	(a period of) grieving.

none • nun

Mrs. Dunn knew a ***nun***, but I knew ***none***.

none	not one.
nun	a woman belonging to a religious order.

one • won

Mr. Dunn ***won*** most of the chess matches we played, having only lost ***one*** match to me.

one	being a single unit.
won	the result of winning.

pail • pale

Gail looked rather ***pale*** this morning as she carried the ***pail*** from the barn.

pail	an open container, especially of metal.
pale	lacking intensity of color.

pain • pane

Jane broke the ***pane*** with her hand, and the ***pain*** is still with her a couple of days later.

pain	an unpleasant sensation caused by the stimulation of certain nerves, especially as a result of an injury.
pane	a single sheet of glass in a window.

pare • pair • pear

Claire used the small knife to ***pare*** her ***pear*** for the ***pair*** of sundaes she was preparing for her mom and herself.

pare	to cut off the out surface, skin, or edge of.
pair	a set of two of the same thing.
pear	a fleshy, juicy, sweet fruit.

passed • past

Cass ***passed*** the photo album to her son and they reminisced about the ***past*** when she, too, ***passed*** her first math quiz.

passed	was marked sufficient for passing an examination or test; to have moved along.
past	just ended.

pause • paws

Paul's dog tracked muddy ***paws*** all over his kitchen floor, and he had to ***pause*** making dinner to clean it up.

pause	a short period of time; to hesitate or stop.
paws	more than one foot of a four-footed animal having claws.

peace • piece

Reese ate a ***piece*** of cake and made ***peace*** with herself for dumping her boyfriend.

peace	a condition when groups are not fighting with one another.
piece	a distinct part.

peak • peek • pique

Monique has a neighbor whose actions in his backyard did ***pique*** her curiosity enough to take a ***peek***, but when she looked and then laughed at the ***peak*** in his yard she did not know her actions would ***pique*** him so.

peak	to become sickly; a pointed top or projection.
peek	to look in such a way as to not be seen.
pique	to cause resentment in by wounding the pride; to stimulate or arouse.

plain • plane

Jane wore a ***plain*** dress on the ***plane*** up to New York, and her ***plain*** manner of speaking gained her new friends on the trip.

plain	simple; easy to see or understand.
plane	one of the main supporting surfaces of an aircraft.

pleas • please

Eloise does not ***please*** the judge as she merely ***pleas*** her mistakes.

pleas	as in s/he gives a statement in court in support of his/her case.
please	to gratify, satisfy, give pleasure to.

pole • poll

Joel took a ***poll*** of the number of accidents involving a ski ***pole***, but found that most of them happened in the north ***pole***.

pole	one of two areas that lie at opposite ends of an axis; a long piece of wood or other material rounded along its length.
poll	the number of votes cast (in an election).

poor • pore • pour

Thor had to ***pore*** over the instructions to determine how much mixture to ***pour*** into the bowl, because he was too ***poor*** to buy more if he made a mistake.

poor	having little money, few possessions, and no luxuries.
pore	to study intently.
pour	to send out in a stream.

presence • presents

Essence was in the ***presence*** of her family when she opened the birthday ***presents*** they bought for her.

presence	the state of being in a certain place.
presents	s/he brings someone or something to the notice of someone else; more than one gift.

principal • principle

Vince's ***principle*** objection was that his child's ***principal*** favored some children over others.

principal	first in importance.
principle	a fundamental implication.

rain • reign • rein

Shayne was a king determined to ***reign*** over his subjects, despite the ***rain***, and he took his horse by the ***rein*** to get to the town square during the storm.

rain	many falling drops of water; to fall like rain.
reign	to hold a royal office or to be a monarch; the power of a monarch.
rein	one of the two strips of leather or rope strapped to the side of a horse's bit.

raise • rays

Mrs. Hayes loved the sun's ***rays*** when they were out, and she made a habit to ***raise*** the shades to enjoy such moments.

raise	to cause to rise or come to a vertical or standing position.
rays	more than one line of light that appears to radiate from some light-producing or light-reflecting object.

read • red

Ned ***read*** his favorite novel by the ***red*** barn.

read	the result of reading.
red	a color.

read • reed

Steve sat near the ***reed*** to ***read*** his favorite novel.

read	to understand the meaning of symbols, signs, gestures, etc.
reed	tall-growing erect grasses found in water or swamps.

real • reel

Neal played the movie ***reel*** of his dad in action as a ***real*** college football star, and his dad was so emotional he began to ***reel*** as he stood.

real	existing in fact; natural.
reel	to sway unsteadily; a revolving device for winding up or letting out yarn, wire, etc.

right • rite • write

Dwight's father taught him ***right*** from wrong so his ***rite*** of passage into manhood was easy.

Dwight went to ***write*** his father a letter using his ***right*** hand as he usually does.

right	true; obeying the moral law; opposite of left.
rite	a religious ceremony.
write	to form letters, figures or other significant symbols, especially on paper, using a pencil, pen, brush etc.

ring • wring

Mrs. Singh took off her ***ring*** just before she started to ***wring*** the towels in order to hang out to dry by the light of sun, and then she went to ***ring*** the outside bell to call her family in for dinner.

ring	to cause a bell to ring; a circular band.
wring	to squeeze and twist so as to force out the moisture.

role • roll

Joel's ***role*** was to bring the ***roll*** out from the back room.

role	the part which an actor or singer is cast in a play, opera, etc.
roll	a quantity of cloth, wrapping paper, etc. rolled up in the form of a cylinder.

ruff • rough

Mr. Gruff thought her cat was playing ***rough*** when it picked up her kitten by its ***ruff***.

ruff	the natural growth of hair or feathers around the neck of a bird or beast.
rough	having a surface which is uneven; turbulent.

sail • sale

Gail made a ***sale*** of a boat to a guy who said he liked to ***sail***.

sail	to travel by boat; a piece of canvas suspended from the spars of a boat or ship to catch or deflect wind.
sale	a selling of.

scene • seen

Jean made a rowdy ***scene*** at the party because she wanted to be ***seen*** in her new pair of jeans.

scene	the place where some event occurs.
seen	having perceived with the eye.

sea • see

Bea wanted to ***see*** what the waves of the ***sea*** looked like in the morning.

sea	the continuous body of salt water covering most of the earth's surface; smaller than an ocean.
see	to perceive with the eye.

seam • seem

Rikeem made a new ***seam*** in his shirt, and he did ***seem*** most impressed with his own handiwork.

seam	a line of stitches.
seem	to give the impression of being something or having a specified attribute.

sew • so

Flo was ***so*** happy to learn how to ***sew*** that she made her father a tie.

sew	to join or fasten by stitches.
so	in a certain way; used to express then.

shore • sure

Gloria was ***sure*** that if she travelled to the ***shore*** in October she would have the boardwalk all to herself.

shore	the land forming the edge of a large expanse of water.
sure	accepted as truth.

soar • sore

Lori stretched her arms out to ***soar*** like a bird, but her sun burnt skin made her arms feel ***sore*** and she yelped in pain.

soar	to rise high in the air.
sore	causing a painful emotion.

sole • soul

Joel's ***sole*** mission, as he tapped the ***sole*** of his shoe on the floor to the beat, was to discover ***soul*** music.

sole	the under surface of (the foot); the only.
soul	the immortal part of man, as distinguished from his body; an emotional expressiveness.

stair • stare

Jerry sat on the bottom ***stair*** outside in order to ***stare*** at his new car.

stair	a constructed step or one of a set of steps by which one can ascend or descend from one level or floor to another.
stare	to look at fixedly.

stake • steak

Jake cooked himself a ***steak*** after driving a ***stake*** in the middle of his back yard.

stake	a length of wood, etc. pointed at one end so as to be driven into the ground and used as a marker.
steak	a thick slice of meat or fish.

stationary • stationery

Patience was ***stationary*** as she thought of what to write on her new ***stationery***.

stationary	not moving.
stationery	writing paper and envelopes.

steal • steel

Neal took the ***steel*** pen thinking it was his; however, when he found out it was not his, he told the true owner he did not mean to ***steal*** the pen.

steal	to take something not rightfully belonging to one.
steel	iron carbide mixed with other metals which is strong in its solid state.

storey • story

Lori lived on the second ***storey*** of her house, and she used the first level to read to the local children one chapter a day from a popular ***story*** book.

storey	one of the floor-to-ceiling portions of a building.
story	an account of a real or imagined event.

straight • strait

Nate traveled the ***strait*** around the bend and then ***straight*** out into the ocean.

straight	having an unchanging direction.
strait	a narrow stretch of water between two land masses.

tacks • tax

Max bought ***tacks*** from the office supply store and paid a ***tax*** of eight percent.

tacks	short, sharp nails; he or she fastens with a tack or tacks.
tax	a charge on a person's income or property.

tail • tale

Gail told the ***tale*** of how her dog chases his ***tail*** every morning as a signal that it's time for a walk.

tail	the part of the body at the lower part of the spine.
tale	an account of a real or imagined event.

taught • taut

Maude ***taught*** her son how to make the rope ***taut*** in order to walk a tight rope routine.

taught	the result of teaching.
taut	under tension.

their • there • they're

Claire and her sister are meeting ***their*** friends at the park over ***there*** where ***they're*** setting up for a barbeque.

their	belonging to or done by them.
there	in or at that place.
they're	they are.

threw • through

Lou accidentally ***threw*** the ball ***through*** the window.

threw	the result of throwing.
through	from one end to the other end of.

thrown • throne

Joan, a princess from Rome, sat on her ***throne*** and watched as the ball was ***thrown*** to her puppy.

thrown	the result of propelling something through the air.
throne	a chair reserved for the use of a sovereign.

thyme • time

Mrs. Rimes used ***thyme*** to flavor her chicken this ***time*** around.

thyme	a fragrant plant used for seasoning in cooking.
time	what a clock measures; a duration.

to • too • two

Lou wanted ***two*** slices of pie, which his mom said was ***too*** much, so instead Lou headed upstairs ***to*** his bedroom to pout.

to	in the direction of; in accompaniment with.
too	excessively; more than is sufficient.
two	being one more that one.

toad • towed

Joe ***towed*** his pet ***toad*** around in a roller skate.

toad	a small, tailless, leaping amphibian with warty skin.
towed	the result of being pulled along with a rope.

told • tolled

Roland was ***tolled*** two dollars this time between his state and the state where his friend lived, so he ***told*** his friend that the price of the toll went up.

told	the result of telling.
tolled	to be taxed or charged a levy.

vane • vein

Shayne installed a weather ***vane*** on top of his roof, and a ***vein*** on his temple grew plump from the effort.

vane	a broad, thin often curved surface fastened to a pivoted or rotating body.
vein	one of the tubular vessels with moderately thin walls that carry blood into a steady stream to and from the heart.

vary • very

Carrie liked ***very*** much to ***vary*** the socks she wore from day to day.

vary	to undergo or introduce change.
very	the same; a high degree; extremely.

wade • weighed

Jade ***weighed*** slightly less now because she liked to ***wade*** in the water for an hour every day.

wade	to walk through some depth of water.
weighed	the result of having determined the weight of.

wail • whale

Gail heard the ***wail*** of a baby ***whale*** that turned up on the beach.

wail	a long drawn-out cry of pain or grief.
whale	a member of many species of immense, fishlike marine mammals.

waist • waste

Macy had a trim ***waist*** because she does not like to ***waste*** her vegetables, choosing to eat them instead.

waist	the narrow part of a human body between the ribs and the hips.
waste	needless and excessive consumption; deterioration or decay by use, misuse or lack of use.

wait • weight

Kate had to ***wait*** as her doctor measured her ***weight***.

wait	to remain in place or in a state of inactivity.
weight	the force acting on a body in the gravitational field.

waive • wave

Mavis decided to ***waive*** her dessert, but she did ***wave*** the waiter over for another soda.

waive	to prefer not to insist on.
wave	an energy-bearing disturbance; to cause to move to and fro with a motion resembling a wave; to make a signal of farewell, welcome.

waiver • waver

Mavis did ***waver*** but she ultimately signed the injury claim ***waiver***, and it was the only way the ski instructor would let her join the class.

waiver	something that represents a preference not to insist on.
waver	to hesitate between a choice.

want • wont

Dante was ***wont*** to be outside, but he did ***want*** to see what the aquarium had to offer.

want	to wish fervently.
wont	a custom or habit; accustomed.

war • wore

Jordan ***wore*** a shirt with an army green pattern even though he was never involved in a ***war***.

war	armed conflict between nations, tribes or other groups.
wore	the result of having on the body; having made unfit for further use.

ware • wear • where

Claire wanted to ***wear*** her sneakers to the antique show, ***where*** she hoped to search the ***ware*** all day for some special items for her home.

ware	goods for sale.
wear	to have on the body; to make unfit for further use.
where	in or at a place.

wax • whacks

Max accidentally ***whacks*** his wrist against the hood of his car just before he goes to ***wax*** it.

wax	to apply wax to; any of various natural or synthetic substances resembling wax in physical or chemical properties of both.
whacks	he or she strikes with a resounding blow.

way • weigh • whey

Fay found a ***way*** to include a good amount of ***whey*** in her meals without having to ***weigh*** the portion in advance.

way	the course taken, or to be taken, in getting from one place to another.
weigh	to determine the weight of.
whey	the watery part of milk left when curds have formed and separated.

weak • week

Tyrique was ***weak*** after being sick last ***week*** so he needed to take some time away from work.

weak	having little physical strength; low in intensity; deficient in mental power.
week	a period of seven days.

weather • whether

Heather couldn't decide ***whether*** the ***weather*** was better for golfing this week or last week.

weather	the atmospheric conditions prevailing at a given place and time.
whether	introducing the first of two or more possibilities.

were • whir

Werner's friends ***were*** about to go home when he caused a model plane to ***whir*** past their heads.

were	to be for they.
whir	to move through the air with a sound resembling that of a bird's wings in rapid flight.

wet • whet

Wesley thought he'd ***whet*** his appetite with some hot wings, but then he had to use a ***wet*** nap to make his fingers less sticky.

wet	to be covered or soaked in water or some other liquid.
whet	to stimulate or arouse.

which • witch

Whitney had an idea about ***which*** neighbor her friend believed was a ***witch*** by the way he described her to Whitney.

which	whatever one or ones.
witch	a woman practicing sourcery.

while • wile

Kyle used his ***wile*** to work his way into the house so he could scope out the items he planned to steal ***while*** he was charming the home owner.

while	during the time that.
wile	a trick using guile so as to deceive.

whine • wine

Kline wanted the ***wine*** so badly that he began to ***whine*** about it.

whine	to complain in a childish way.
wine	a drink made of the fermented juice of grapes.

whirled • world

Worthington had a replica of the ***world*** called a globe that he ***whirled*** as fast as it would go.

whirled	the result of having revolved rapidly.
world	the planet earth.

whirred • word

Werner was having a ***word*** with his dad on the porch when his brother's model helicopter suddenly ***whirred*** overhead.

whirred	the result of having moved through the air with a sound of a bird's wings in rapid flight.
word	a speech sound or combination of sounds having meaning and used as a basic unit of language and human communication.

who's • whose

Judy is a woman ***who's*** friends with a man ***whose*** mother is a princess.

who's	what or which person is.
whose	belonging to a person.

wood • would

Woody ***would*** like to learn how to whittle a block of ***wood***.

wood	the hard substance comprising the largest part of stems and branches of trees and shrubs.
would	used to express the future in indirect terms; the past tense of will.

you're • your

Eunice told me that ***you're*** having a bit of trouble working through all of ***your*** arithmetic homework.

you're	you are.
your	belonging to you.

Index of Word Groups

Intellectually Competitive Edge, Inc.
thanks you for purchasing and using
this edition of ***Homophone
Words That Sound Alike***.

Printed in Great Britain
by Amazon